The End of American Liberty

Freedom of Speech, Gun Rights, and Other Liberties are Threatened in the Next Election

I0414716

T. H. Logwood

" Liberty has it's price, Freedom it's costs, and elections have consequences."

Our Freedoms and Liberties are Fragile

Among the greatest of attributes of America are the Rights and Freedoms guaranteed under the Constitution. We enjoy many liberties and opportunities that most other countries do not offer their citizens, but that is changing in America. There are so many great and generally overlooked or unappreciated freedoms we have, so often taken for granted. Not that America is a utopian nation by any means, with many challenges to overcome, but it remains a "work in progress", ever changing. Still, this country offers the most and best to its citizens, more than any country ever in the history of man. So why would anyone want to change it, or take away our liberties?

Sadly, there is a great and increasingly powerful movement to destroy America, by stripping away our Rights and Freedoms. The plan is to replace individual liberty with government dependency, a utopian society where everything is "free and fair to all". Government knows best, government is the answer for every need in life, and it should be decided and controlled by an elite group of intellectuals, who are best able to meet the needs of the common people. If history wasn't erased or twisted in our radicalized public school systems, then that would read exactly from the Stalinist manifesto (aka: Socialism 101).

Socialism is not a good thing for a nation, it destroys it. Those that profess its wonders are the "radical left", "liberals", "globalists", and "elitists", that say "if socialism is done right, everybody is equal, everything is fair, free this, free that, and so on." In a perfect utopian fantasy world, where unicorns fly, perhaps so, but socialism just does not work. No country (or its citizens) have ever prospered from this ideology, none. Because history in our schools is being changed, each new crop of graduates is more accepting and in-step with such thinking.

Does anyone remember World War II, and the fight against fascism and socialism? What happened to Cambodia under the rule of Paul Pott and the "red shirts"? Look at every example, like current Venezuela; how well has socialism worked for them? Socialism means taking away personal liberties, freedoms, and choice, and allowing a select few government bureaucrats to make all of the decisions for the populace. "Power given to a few, always turns corrupt, they abuse it, opposition is eliminated, and the nation is destroyed". There have been no exceptions.

During the 1940s and 50s, fascism, socialism, and communism, were dark and dirty words. Americans celebrated life, valued family and worship, shunned violence, and were abhorrent to the mention of demonology. The "Big" war was over, and the enemies of the freedom loving people were defeated, although communism was on the rise. Life in America turned from war production, to the greatest buildup of wealth and material goods the world had ever seen. America was the leader in protecting freedom and the rights of individual citizens, and the prosperity we had was evidence of that.

The 1960s and 70s was a time of revolutions, drastic changes in social norms and acceptances, as the world again sunk into global conflicts and unrest. The "young generation" sought to rebel, turning away from social norms, for a more "liberated" radical freedom of self-expression and thought. American society was changing, pushed by radical thinkers professing violent action to solve the perceived injustices of the day. But as the revolts did not materialize, the radicals got smart and blended into the society they hoped to overthrow. Why? In the land of plenty, the "have- nots" wanted something they were not getting?

It was noted by a former Soviet official, that "they can flip a country into a socialist State in three years". America could not be defeated by military might, but it can be toppled by changing the mindset. Infiltrate the education system and reeducate the children into acceptance of alternate thinking. Control the media, including film, to spew propaganda to the masses. Then from the ranks of zombies, get them elected into public office and the courts to legitimize and solidify the socialist dogma. Get the people to become addicted to handouts, freebies, and the idea that government is their provider.

Those radicalized during the social upheaval, became teachers and professors, went into film and the media (notably the news media), and have spent the last fifty years or so, culturing new generations of social radicals, those that would question and fight the social norms. Look at America now, it seems we are sinking ever deeper in the cesspool of depravity.

This is now evident in today's culture, where all of the normal traditional values are turned topsy-turvy. What was bad is now hailed as good, and everything good is now called racist, old-fashioned, or has a label with a "phobia" attached on the end. The younger generations are schooled by ever more socialistic thinking teachers, which is a byproduct of the 60s revolutionaries.

The guise of "fairness', "saving the environment", open borders, and the merits of socialism are ever present in today's media, and professed by more and more politicians. America celebrates death instead of life, with the murder rate of about 60 million (aborted) babies since Roe v. Wade. The traditional family, and the merits of individualism, is being replaced by government programs, with the intent of government providing "All of our needs". As more people get hooked on government handouts and programs, taxes increase, and personal choices decline. This is the path to socialism, which leads to the end of personal freedoms and liberties, resulting in a communist society where there are no Rights.

Everything in America is under attack these days. What was right is now wrong. Even monuments of our past heroes and events are under attack by those wishing to change our history. Not only have the schoolbooks been changed to a "more friendly" and "alternate reality" of what really happened, the social elites are tearing down historical markers, monuments, and changing the names on streets and buildings. This has been particularly true with many of the American Civil War memorabilia, like the Southern Battle flag, and Southern statues of leaders and memorials. History happened, and defaming the events doesn't change the realities. History taught in our public school system is not what it used to be. As the social warriors erase the events, our children are not taught our heritage, and the road we struggled to get to this very point. History is a great teacher for a nation. If you fail to teach history, you will repeat it.

Of Rights and Freedoms

Now understand there are differences between Rights, Freedoms, and Liberties. A Right, is a constitutionally guaranteed action or principle, the basis and fundamental to every American citizen. A Freedom and Liberty are really the same, in that, it reflects the personal and non-coerced option of choice. To be able to choose freely, over nearly every aspect of daily life, is a freedom and liberty coveted by the world, yet taken for granted by Americans.

Our freedoms and rights have not been easily gained, bathed in blood and struggle against tyranny and forces always seeking to restrict and limit them. For over 200 years, from the American Revolution against English tyranny, to the wars and conflicts today have been waged to keep and maintain our rights and freedoms. Our young men (and women) have sacrificed their all in the defense of our freedoms. It is said of the innumerable battles fought for our liberty, "Who remembers the names? Only those who fought there, those who bled there, and those that died there." This is the American story, the realities of forming and preserving a nation of freedom, and it is important our story is taught to our children. It is critical that they learn our past, so perhaps they can learn from the past what works or fails, and how to make better choices.

The struggles continue today, more so from within our country, by our own people, to take our freedoms away. Why? Is it such a bad thing to have the freedoms to choose for yourself what to eat, what to wear, what to drive, where to live, what kind of work to do to earn wages, and so on? Is it so wrong to say something out loud that you don't like? It has been our right from the beginning of this country to speak out, debate, and seek compromise. Yet, there is a great movement of people and leaders enacting laws to restrict our voice.

What is happening to this country? Strife and conflict seems to be rampant throughout every part of our society, the political process is full of anger and crooked activities, and we seem to be a people divided along racial and ideological lines. What is going on?

Just a few years ago, even talk of the positive attributes of socialism was rare, and never mentioned during an election bid. But now, many candidates running for national office, even the highest office, the presidency, openly tout the promises and benefits of socialistic ideals. Something has changed in America, and not for the better.

America, founded with the ideals of personal liberties and rights guaranteed by the Constitution, individualism and hard work, freedom of speech and worship, family, and the capitalist model for nation building, have all radically changed. The very core of every traditional value and precept of what America is (or was), is becoming something very different, and not in a positive way.

There are groups and individuals, and great forces at work in this country (and outside the borders), trying to destroy America, seeking to turn it into a third-world socialist nation. A nation where a select group, the Elites, rule over every aspect of our lives, from our speech, what is taught in our schools to our children, what we do for work, what we should think, even what we should eat. After all, as a people, we can not make our own decisions, because these elitists are smarter than we are. They know better on how we should take care of ourselves, and how we should interact among our comrades. Who are these people?

Who are these people? Call them leftists, elites, progressives, radicals, and so on, but it is very clear who they are. They are the "left wing" of the democrat party, who shouts for fairness and equality. It is the social warriors of Hollywood and the media that speaks of the "racism" in this country. They are the school teachers and college professors that erase and change history to something other than reality. It is the mobs of brain-washed young people marching in violent riots across the country demanding "the flavor of the day" hysteria. It is those screaming for radical changes to norms and tradition.

The Elites are all of those that say things and seek to enact rules and laws to take away your freedom to make your own choices. They are the ones restricting the words you choose to speak, and constantly trying to make everything from jobs and wages to education, fair for everyone, a "level playing field". These people are the ones that seek higher taxation to fund ever expanding government programs to redistribute resources to those they deem "unfairly treated" by certain groups of society.

The elitists are typically wealthy, and often famous, in positions of power or prominence, where they gain a public spotlight to express what should be done to make things "fair". Some of these elites are very quiet and very powerful manipulators working in the background to bring about changes. They are all socialists, and hypocrites. Hypocrites because they talk of making everything fair, "taking from the rich to give to the poor", but yet, they squawk when they are asked to give their fair share. "Raise everyone's taxes, but don't touch my stash."

Again, to be made plain and clear, what is happening is that these loud-mouth social-warriors are trying to change America. Change America into a socialist state where individual thought and liberty is tightly controlled. It is just as the former Soviet official had explained, that a nation could be toppled in a few years by following a fairly simple formula. "You infect every part of society, and the highest levels, where policies, laws, and rules can be changed. Strip away rights, and replace it with government programs and laws. Educate the young into thinking State-first, and minimize individual merit." It is a long-term plan for change, and with each election, more politicians are elected that support these ideals.

The Last Election

The next election may well be the last free election we have in this country. Our liberties and rights are slipping away with every election cycle, and soon, our freedom of speech (expressed through our vote) may disappear. Once our ability to speak freely is gone, then all of our other rights will be silenced as well. This is become more true as "hate speech laws", and other legislation is enacted, to promote "tolerance" and "fairness for all". The cost is limiting the free expression of thoughts and ideas, and the ability to condemn or condone such.

Strong words and a bold statement, but it may be very true as we watch and wrestle with the political and legal events as these weeks and months lead up to the next key election. Watching the 2018 mid-term elections, the trend and precursor for the next cycle is clear. Rather, the trend is scary. Opinion surveys and many commentators suggest that socialism and socialistic ideals are acceptable, and even desirable, particularly with younger adults. If the next generation, our youth and young adults, are so swayed by the promises of "free stuff" and "the government will take care of you", then we are in grave danger indeed. What politician's promise, government begrudgingly gives. And what the government gives, it can also take it away.

Remember the 2018 mid-term election? What was at stake, and who showed up to vote? The rhetoric and saber-rattling from both the republican and democrat sides, coupled with the endless blabbering dribble from the biased media, spelled out clearly the goals of the both parties. The independent voters decided the vote, and the preservation of this country's liberties continued. But for how much longer? What will happen in 2020, and 2024? Consider each candidate, and where they stand on personal rights and liberties, versus government control. Who benefits, and what are their underlying motives?

At stake during the 2018 election, according to the pro-republican stance, was stability and legality. Under the strong leadership of President Trump, the economy has blossomed to an unfathomable growth rate around 4% (give or take a smidge) almost immediately after he took office. He kept his campaign promises of bringing at least one (now two) "Originalist" supreme court justices to the bench, repealed piles of burdensome and ridiculous government regulations, restored the rule of law (especially with regards to immigration), and prevented disastrous world conflicts such as with North Korea, Russia, and Iran. He upheld constitutional rights and principles, affirmed the right to life and the right to bear arms, among many other bold actions. The republican platform was to keep moving in this direction, build on job growth and the economy, following the "rule of law", fix the illegal alien and immigration mess, and restore civility among our divided peoples.

Looking back on the many and great accomplishments of President Trump, America is in much better condition, perhaps more traditional, like during the earlier eras. There is more personal choice and liberties, less government control, more jobs, and renewed world respect. Aren't these good things?

Now without question, the democrat side clearly fought for the opposite platform. It can be clearly shown that there was never a single mention of policy, or what they would do to improve the lives of Americans. They took a different approach, and showed truly what the new democrat party stood for. Their intent was to unravel and destroy every positive action President Trump has accomplished. They yelled out hate-speech towards anything of growth, improvement, or prosperity. They shouted out "phobia hysteria," talked about impeaching the newly appointed justice to the supreme court, and shouted down anyone who would not get on their "bandwagon". Many in congress writhed with hatred and made idle threats of impeaching President Trump himself. These elected democrats cried and had temper-tantrums about anything related to the mass invasion by illegal aliens. Never once, did any democrat candidate talk about "How" they would fix health care, restore jobs for Americans, do better with our international responsibilities, and so on.

Ok, if you are unhappy with a policy or action, tell us in clearly, without the emotional drama, of "what" you would do differently. Their entire political strategy was to slander and malign anyone and everything that was that contrary to their anti-American hate-filled dialogue. Even the mainstream media, heavily biased against the president, was in lock-step with the democrat mob mentality. Is the new democrat party truly representative of all democrats?

And who showed up to vote in 2018?

"It's that time again, elections." To some it's dread and bother, a disruption in the daily routine, so too many people just don't vote. To others, it is an opportunity for gain and advancement, propelling an agenda, or other ends. Whatever the motives, or lack of motives, the bottom line is this, we have a Right and a privilege to choose leaders in this country. Our Right is different than in most other countries in the world, because our election process is still free from the interference of government. Not many nations of the world can claim that. Certainly there is graft and corruption, and the lobbying of special interests that can influence "how" we vote, but the process itself is still relatively the same as our founding fathers intended it long ago.

In the 2018 mid-term election cycle, the democrats made a strong showing, with a fairly high voter turnout. What the party had done very well, was to mobilize their campaigns, with workers and volunteers, that actively encouraged people to vote. Overall, the democrat machine was well tuned, enthusiastic, and passionate, resulting in a good turnout. Despite some of the questionable tactics and methods to get people registered and voted, "the process" of promoting the freedom to vote earns the party a resounding "Kudos". The exit polling showed a very strong young adult block, but decreased voting from the African-American group, and Hispanic voters.

Mid-aged suburban white women seemed to strongly support the republican candidates, as did increased voters among the Black and Hispanic communities. It is quite likely that many voters were encouraged to vote "against" the constant maligning of the Kavanaugh appointment, many being former democrats. The greatly improved job situation also prompted minorities to "vote red". The traditional white male voter, backbone of the republican party, actually was down from the 2016 presidential election.

Overall, the republicans made a weak and pathetic showing in many of the races. They were slow and lacking in messaging, showed little passion, and the underlying sentiment was, "who cares". The results were appalling for a party that gained so much just two years earlier when they overwhelmingly elected Trump, "the Outsider".

The result of the 2018 mid-term election was a radical change in Congress, where the democrats, led by Nancy Pelosi taking control. Instead of working for positive changes, implementing plans and programs for the people, they have spent every taxpayer dollar to disrupt the presidents actions to improve the lives of the people. Nancy and the democrats initiated wasteful and needless investigations, endless political posturing, spewing hatred and discourse, almost inciting revolution, instead of serving the citizens, which they have sworn to serve. Elections have consequences.

The importance of your vote, which is your voice, should be expressed, and especially for the upcoming election. If you can physically do so, do vote. Whether you like a particular candidate or party, or a proposed law that's on a ballot, let your voice be heard. You have the right not to vote, and that is a free decision for you to determine. But not to vote, is surrendering your voice to the outcome of those that did cast their ballots.

As our society writhes with turmoil and unrest, the forces of change come about, heading towards a revolution or major upheaval of our liberties. And in this country, at this moment in time, many of these groups, will further seek to undermine our rights to vote, our power to voice our opinion, and that would sound the death-blow to America. If our speech (and the choices made through voting) is restricted or controlled by laws and deceitful leaders, then the path to a socialistic, and then a totalitarian country will be complete.

Voting is a Right and Privilege

Vote, or not, it is your decision, but it far more important than you can imagine. It is your Right, and duty, as a citizen to change the face of the governing bodies, if you so choose. The process of voting came about in this country because of the forced hand of the English crown to dictate almost every facet of the lives of the colonial governed. The idea of the government controlling everything in the lives of the early Americans became intolerable to the point of the revolution. Over 200 years later, do we as a nation want to go back to everything being government controlled?

In the new land, the New World, the colonies were largely established to be free of the dictates of their rulers in England. It was often related to spiritual choice and expression, that led groups to the new world seeking some relief from the overlords of government interference with their beliefs and speech, especially when contrary to government actions. The new land meant a certain amount of liberty to express thoughts and ideas, and the election process if not borne, was greatly fostered.

It was greatly due to the interference of the governing bodies in the daily affairs of the colonists, which dissention grew and eventually turned to rebellion, hence the revolution of liberty had come about. Authority over our lives is contrary to our innate sense of freedom and independence.

The founding fathers were absolutely brilliant in their crafting of the constitution, especially in regards to setting up the system of voting. They clearly understood what it meant to have a voice, to be able to freely express an opinion or idea without being arrested or suppressed by those in power. Certainly there are great dissertations of how the system of voting came about, but the point being, it did, and is meant so the common man (now including women) can have some say in how their lives would be governed.

The Constitution

Nicely written and clearly defined in the remarkable document, the US Constitution is nothing short of a miraculous template of how to govern a people. Now, one of the chief cornerstones of the constitution, and basic law of the land, is that there are to be periodic elections, free from government interference, for the people to select among themselves the next body of leaders. That is, freely held elections for various offices and levels of government, free from the coercion or compulsion by the government or other persons.

Without this privilege, there is no liberty. It takes time back to the pre-revolutionary days where the government would control what you said, what you did, and all other aspects of life. Without the freedom to choose for ourselves, there is no incentive to improve ones life. Power in the hands of a few elites, has never worked out well for any country, throughout all of human history. What happens in every nation, documented throughout history, is that power corrupts. As power becomes concentrated in the hands of a few, they abuse it. Then the rulers oppress the people. Finally, due to opposition, the rulers mass murder their own citizens to maintain their power. Gratefully, our Founders divided the centers of powers, each as a check upon the other.

A people that are free to decide for themselves are happier in their daily lives, more productive, which makes the nation great and prosperous as a whole. That is it in a nutshell, a free people are happier and more productive. And that is the intent of the constitution.

On the federal level, the founding fathers intended that the government's primary role and duty was to provide for the common defense of the nation, and, support the common good. Without defense of the nation, when needed, such as by a foreign invader, then a nation is overrun and destroyed. The Founders understood this all too well in those early times, so in a simplistic but exacting manner, they crafted the document to make provisions for the armed and legal protections for the country. This included, if you study the document, for maintaining and defending the borders. A nation has the sovereign Right to have borders, which is the government's top priority.

Along with national defense, the Founders tried to instill the idea that if people are left to their own means, they will create jobs and businesses (commerce), for which families and society can provide for their own needs, hence a healthier country. With increased governmental interference in the lives of people, happiness and productivity declines. So the document intended to be in support of the "good works" that people would do, rather than government controlling the daily aspects of life. "The pursuit of happiness" as it reads, means for the government to not interfere with the lives of the people. Laws and rules certainly are needed to govern and maintain the rights and liberties of society, but not into every decision of our personal lives.

Now over two hundred years later, the heavy hand of government has burdened us all with endless regulations, restrictions, and controls, impeding the happiness and contentment of the governed. Granted, as our society has changed and developed, a certain amount of governmental control is obviously necessary, but as the government continues to grow, the bureaucracy has strangled many of our rights and privileges, including our freedom of speech.

The Political Divide

Today, right now in America, there are groups that are trying to prevent your freedom of speech to be heard. There are many forces at work to strip away the rights and freedoms we hold, that are sanctioned by our constitutional foundations. Should I name them? They are in every slanderous news and media agency, half of the current governing body, and the various groups shouting and pillaging as they attempt to suppress thought.

Groups like the "Me Too", "Women's March", "Antifa", "the Awake (or Awoke) Movement", "Black Lives Matter", and others, profess tolerance and inclusiveness, but truly are not. Hailed and supported by the bias distorting media, these groups preach fairness, while seeking to tear away at personal liberties and rights. If one disagrees to them, what happens? These groups shout, scream, and take violent actions against any dissent with "their" thinking. And then there are scores of lawyers waiting to file legal proceedings to support their censorship actions.

This is increasingly more common, as Stalinist tactics are used to push a darker agenda. Freedom to speak out, and freedom to assemble, are core Rights under our system, but disagreement and obverse thought are also guaranteed. Suppression via slander or violence are never acceptable, yet that is what these groups commonly use. Censorship is not just of the written word, but it also applies to anything verbally spoken. If you speak out against the latest riots for instance, you're called a "racist", and groups will hunt you down and threaten your well being.

Yes, speak out, let your voice be heard with truth or opposing thoughts, but without oppression. That is, if we are adults, let us discuss and reason as adults. When one shouts and fusses, then it is that inner child that needs a "time-out", or maybe a solid spanking. If you don't have anything substantive to offer, then screaming and potty-mouth babble will never sway a debate. For many in our media and leadership roles, they act more like nasty children, than people we should follow or admire.

"When all else fails - scream the race card"

If you disagree with the thinking of these zombie-like groups, they will shout you down, or take legal, and sometimes violent actions to silence thought. Watching groups or mobs march down the streets crying and wailing as they throw rocks and destroy property, screaming hateful insults, really does not help their cause. How many news stories and reports has been just that, mob violence, yet the media condones it as "peaceful protests". As elections get closer, the divisive rhetoric and violence increases. Is that the new normal for American expression or speech? At what point does freedom of speech end? The answer is, when the rights of another is limited or effected.

It is fair to disagree and oppose the thoughts and ideas of someone else, that is our Right. If you don't want to listen, that is your right. If you disagree, that is your right. If you want to speak to the contrary and try to persuade others in thinking the same, that is your right also. But is there a line that cannot or should not be crossed? Yes. When you limit and prevent someone else from their rights, that must not happen. Your right is to speak freely, without governmental interference, or other parties suppressing your voice. That is how our fundamental laws work (or suppose to work). The rule of law tells us, that "one persons rights end when it interferes with another's".

If there is an alternate or opposing viewpoint on a subject, then can we not sit down together and reason? In a society where media and a wide diversity of peoples and opinions abound, there should be great ideas and discussions of every topic and idea to enrich and improve our lives.

What we see is the contrary, where the media is controlled by biased deceitful owners and executives, that seek revenues by a ratings ranking system, hence controlling what the public will view. It is money that drives the media, emotions that fuels the information presented, and the control of free and open speech is the result. The "mainstream" media, the newspapers, tv, radio, and internet, are no longer "fair and unbiased". For the most part, they are greatly controlled by a few powerful moguls, which control the content and narrative they want to promote. Over the past few years, they have shown how corrupt and disgraceful they have become. That is why they are referred to as the "fake news".

The freedom of speech relates exactly to the freedom and right to vote. If your vote elects leaders that uphold the rule of law, then they are apt to uphold the free dissemination of speech. If you are prevented from voting, intimated, threatened with violence or governmental control, your rights to speak out, through the casting of a vote, that is wrong. It is a violation of the most basic of American freedoms, and that must never be allowed to happen. But it has happened, and is happening in many precincts and places where people are suppose to be allowed to freely assemble and cast their voice.

If poor leaders are elected to office, then they will enact more laws and regulations to limit your freedom of expression, even voting. And what was the basic of all basic American privileges, becomes a memory. With every regulation and law that limits what we can and can not do as a free people, then our liberties disappear. We as a people sink into the historical abyss of government controlling everything, and there is no more freedom. This is also exactly true of every right and freedom guaranteed by our constitution.

The New Democrat Party

The new democrat party aligns itself to bold speech with no substance. Violent and divisive rhetoric to stir up the masses of brainwashed supporters to overthrow society, on every issue of tradition, the rule of law, and personal freedom. The new party professes the goodness of socialistic ideals, but white-washes the realities of repeated historical failures. They preach tolerance and fairness, only as long as you agree with their radical agendas. "Condemnation without solution", is the tactic. The "peoples party" is no longer the party of the people, but by the party leadership pushing to overturn the rights of free speech, the rule of law, for an "equality for all" doctrine. They are indoctrinating of our school children with the idea that "government provides" versus hard work and achievement by merit. This is fact.

In fact, the leftist control of the democrat party embraces the Black Lives Matter (BLM) movement. According the BLM website, they openly profess being a Marxist organization, where violence and chaos is their means to promote their demands. And if you read the hatefulness on their website, it is a wonder why the authorities doesn't arrest everyone of them! They are all about overthrowing this government, destroying all of the norms and traditional values America has stood for, violence and mayhem, and so on. Yet the democrat party strongly aligns themselves with this dangerous terrorist gang.

Today's democrat party is far different than the party of years past. In the last election, and as the next election cycle approaches, the New Democrat Party has become "radically left", that is, extreme in their platform of ideals that is suppose to represent the party as a whole. If this is not so, where is the opposition within the party to offer other viewpoints? It is said by some commentators, that "the new party is 2/5ths radical hard-core crazy socialists, 2/5ths are the silent middle, and 1/5th is the more conservative Kennedy-era democrats." Because they fear the left, the moderates and conservatives remain silent, so the party has platform has become pure lunacy.

Currently, the leftist controlled democrat party professes some destructive ideas. The leadership and many of the candidates and supporters profess ever bigger government, higher taxation of the "wealthy" and corporations (70% and 90%, respectively) to subsidize more and larger government redistribution programs. Taxation is the way to pay for programs and handouts, "leveling the playing field for everyone". They then want open national borders where everyone is welcome, where each person will be given services and financial support. That does happen now, but the influx of people into the country could easily be millions. They want free education, especially at the collegiate level, along with government-sponsored free health care. Increased social security benefits to everyone, including "a woman's right to choose an abortion on demand" (even after birth). Changing the Constitution to eliminate the electoral college, so that "democracy" chooses the leaders, along with eliminating gun ownership, among other colorful changes. And the latest is the "Green New Deal", which will save the planet from imminent destruction. The resounding theme is that personal choice and liberty is better served by government edict.

Perhaps some or all of these goals sound good (on the surface), and should be done to make America better, but learn more of how and what that really entails. How to implement these ideas is where debate and discussion should happen, at least in the media which is suppose to be fair and unbiased. Reality and rational thinking is apparently something to be ignored by the democrats. There is just no money to pay for all of this stuff, even to tax every working American 100%! These proposed programs would cost tens of Trillions of dollars at the very least.

Free stuff just does not happen, it costs somebody something. Free education costs a lot, it is not free. Who pays? Increased taxes for all to send some else's kids to college, fair or right? Free heath care? A return to the disastrous Obama/Biden failure of the "Un-Affordable Health Care Act" is nothing more than insanity. That program alone wasted hundreds of Billions of taxpayer dollars, and robbed Social Security, in order to give fewer people poorer health coverage than before. It was considered a "tax" by a socialist biased Supreme Court ruling, now overturned as unconstitutional. It is tragic that a woman may have to choose between having a baby or not, but where is the outcry from groups like Black Lives Matter and the ACLU, when it is minority babies that are slaughtered. It is a double standard, controlled by a few elites making all the decisions for the masses.

And the immigration issue isn't fairly or openly discussed either. A nation is a nation because of its borders and controlling who comes into it. No other country in the world has open borders. The European Union (EU) has largely done away with the national boundaries, but at the cost of national sovereignty and rights. Europe right now is a mess, in every aspect. In America, it is the primary role of the president and the national government to protect the borders and the citizenry. Study the U.S. Constitution. And then to give new immigrants services and financial support? That comes from our taxes and paychecks, is that right? America needs to take care of the needs of its own people before mindlessly admitting the masses into "our" nation.

And the notion the this Green New Deal will save the planet, is pure fantasy from Hollywood and the Unicorn Utopians of Shangri La-La Land. As originally stated on the democrat website, the program would end all use of steel, glass, and cars, eliminate cows and hogs (because of the methane gases they produce). Oil and coal (the backbone of the world's energy) would be replaced by solar and wind-generated energy. Every building will be remodeled to super energy efficiency, and high-speed trains to everywhere. And if you don't want to work, the government will give you a check. Ponder these ideas, and consider the realities. It is not possible under any scenario, and then our current economy would become more like Venezuela or Ethiopia, no money, no work, no anything except repressive government control.

This radical departure of party norms relates exactly to every election, where more and more districts and States are turning democrat blue. Turning blue, not by advancing sound policies and programs to make positive changes (as they offer none), but more so accomplished through unrealistic ideals and false promises. The general populace is being brainwashed by empty rhetoric that touts provision (through increased taxation and control), and unsubstantiated opinion and emotional outbursts, over logic and reason. Yet the vote turns blue, in more and more areas. The power of the individual is given over to mass hysteria. All power is given over to a handful of people, versus the tradition of hard work, individual achievement, and the free marketplace to find real solutions for the challenges facing our ever-changing society.

If this country is to be changed, let it be changed, but through the process of law as it was founded. But what is changed, may not be what is good or right, or even fair. And what changes, is not easily changed back. If traditions are deemed wrong, and what we have previously known as failed ideologies can become entrenched as doctrine. Then individual liberties are restricted, the rule of law becomes contrary to those established by our forefathers, and power becomes concentrated in the hands of a few. In other words, a socialist country.

And power in the hands of a few, ruins nations. It is said, that "power leads to a hunger for more", like any addictive drug. "Once those who thirst for power instead of service, attain power, they start to abuse it. As the abuse and corruption increases, then oppression of opposition begins. And the historical factual reality is then, citizens are mass murdered by their own government." They start with eliminating the opposition, then they turn to the media and professors that initially supported the radicalization. Look at every socialist or totalitarian country, and count the bodies.

In recent times, just look at what happened to: Nazi Germany, Spain, Italy, and Japan of the World War II era, the failure of the Soviet Union, Cambodia under Paul Pott, Argentina, Chile, Venezuela, many other nations throughout South America and Africa. Power corrupts, and the only way to stop the opposition is to remove them. That is the historical reality in every case. The idea that socialism can work is wrong. It only brings a nation, and its citizens, to ruin.

Who, or what groups adhere to what you hold as good and right? What you believe in, and the rights and privileges you enjoy, are just a few votes away from being changed. Think for yourself, and decide in the way that works best for you. Align yourself with those that hold those principles and ideals you want. It doesn't matter which party, just learn who the candidates are, and support those that have the values and principles that you value.

The Hate Trump Movement

One of the greatest privileges this country offers, is free and open elections. By constitutional law, this country is to have free and fair elections, whereby the governed will periodically elect its leaders from their peers, in a peaceful transition of power. And for the most part, for over 200 years, our system of elections and voting is fairly honest. The outcomes are sometimes a question, and when one side loses, they lick their wounds, get on with business, and plan for the next election. At least, that is how it should be.

Remember the 2016 presidential election? It turned a new chapter in American politics, where the outsiders were favored over the mainstream candidates. It was also characterized by hate-speech, threats, temper-tantrums, protest marches, and a bias inflammatory media spreading yellow journalism the likes of which parallels pre-war Nazi Germany. The democrats could not stand the fact, literally the fact, that Donald J. Trump was elected president, over their deceptive and depraved failure in Ms. Clinton and the media propaganda machine.

Who is Donald J. Trump anyways? Outsider, businessman, real estate tycoon, playboy, TV star, republican, moderate conservative, a disrupter of the status quo, and a nationalist. Who in their right mind would have ever guessed that "He" would become president, leader of the free world, defender of the Constitution, and for now, has brought a halt to the national decay this country has had. Against all odds, he won, and the leftist party of the democrats hasn't accepted this reality, even to this very moment. And they never will. Elections have consequences, and this is part of the process. The republican party didn't throw such a tizzy after Obama/Biden got elected.

Not only the democrats, but the republican "Rhinos" and "Never-Trumpers", the entrenched "Swamp Rats" of the DC power cesspool, all have been against him ever since his announcement to run for president. It isn't just a dislike for the president, but hatred as for everything that he is, and stands for. These are the power-hungry wanna-be leaders, seeking to control the masses with their own sick propaganda of "One-Worldism" and global control. The power elites have been seeking control for decades, with the aim of destroying the constitution, and all of the freedoms granted therein.

President Trump stands for our constitution, the rule of law, rights and freedoms, "America-first", strong armed forces, secure borders, a robust economy, individual liberty and choices, and a government "hands-off" policy. And the left progressives hates this. Are you better off than you were before he took office? Then why would anyone want change this, except for greedy selfish ambitions of something sinister?

Even in the political volleying today, over the border wall and security, the most vile and deceptive leaders, Nancy Pelosi (Majority Leader in the house) and Chuck Schumer (Senate Minority Leader), have shown what's in their hearts, hatred of America. They have a hatred towards the president, hatred of the constitution, hatred of truth and fairness, and hatred of the free people that side with the president. If politics and the control of the masses are more important than doing what is right and best for the nation, then those types of leaders need to be voted out of office. What type of leaders do we want in office? Do they serve the people, or line their own pockets? Do they support the rule of law and the constitution, or protect rights and liberties?

President Trump is not the issue, it's what he has done and what he hopes to accomplish that the Trump-Haters oppose. Those things are the Constitution, the rule of law, enforcing the laws, rights and liberties. In a society where government holds the power and makes decisions on behalf of the people, free speech is not tolerated, the good of the people is marginalized, and the health and productivity of the nation is stifled. "Power held in the hands of a few, will bring ruin to a nation." That cannot be emphasized enough.

The Media - Free Speech or Not?

Rights, freedom, and liberty, has ever been the cornerstone of having a free and uncensored press. Until the advent of the radio and tv, newspapers were the primary media to spread news and information. Certainly now with the internet, social-media is a huge vehicle for sharing news and ideas. But has it changed?

What was the journalist's creed of investigating and reporting factual information, has given way to bias slander and "yellow journalistic politics". Many in today's media hide behind the First Amendment's protection of free speech, even though it may be false, misleading, or without fact or evidence. Instead of sharing information and facts in a neutral manner, the media has become highly politicized and biased. It has been widely proven time and time again, the major media and news organizations have lied and manipulated important stories to fit their anti-Trump agenda. Proven facts about the whole Russian collusion scandal, the fake impeachment debacle, and the violent riots in our cities, are grossly and blatantly misrepresented.

To this point, it has been the freedom of speech, and freedom of the press, which has helped to balance the rule of government, being a "check" on the concentration of power by government. In our free and open society, where speech is suppose to be open and nearly unrestricted, the media has been an important and key factor in assuring our liberties. But the media can be used to manipulate the people also.

Media is a tool to reach the masses with whatever information they wish to promote. During the World War II era, the Nazi controlled government used the media to spew its biased propaganda to support it's obscene objectives. The Japanese did the same, followed by the communists under Stalin, and the Chinese under Mao Tse-tung. The media can be a powerful tool for the good of the people, or for the power of the few. And true, our government used the media during World War II to support the war effort, that added some bias, but it was to support personal freedom, not restrict it.

In more recent years, especially during and since the 2016 election, the media has been overly biased and inaccurate, and strongly in opposition to President Trump. The media has been taken over by elitists that seeks the downfall of nationalism and personal liberty. In the past, where laws of slander would prompt fair and accurate reporting, they now purposely malign anything positive the president has accomplished. In fact, the media largely does not report any of the many positive things he has done. Rather, they promote false and biased stories, often without checking the sources or accuracy.

Among the many examples where the major tv and newspaper outlets have not covered the truthful stories or events has been with the numerous Obama/Biden scandals, the Clinton email and dirty dealings cover-ups, the Clinton-Russian tampering in the 2016 election, the egregious investigations into the Trump election, among others. In the past where the news media would usually offer fair and honest investigated and substantiated reporting. They are now a propaganda arm of the democrat party.

A good example of the false and misleading bias of the mainstream media is about President Trump and his use of trade tariffs. The president, who is a highly successful businessman, knows how to make deals, and has done so with foreign governments. One technique is to use tariffs as a negotiating tool. Tariffs are a tax on imported goods from another nation. It can protect a few major businesses, but results in higher costs for goods to the consumer. Overall, implementing tariffs are bad for the consumer, but they can be used as a leveraging tool in diplomacy.

One of President Trump's key negotiations has been with China, our largest trading partner. Since then President Nixon opened the dealings with China in 1968, the Chinese has abused and used our open society to lie, cheat, and steal from American businesses. President Trump uses trade tariffs to leverage our position to change China's practices. Tariffs are a tool, not greatly good for the consumer, but if done right, can force the opponent to handle trade differently. That is exactly what the president has done, but the media "black-balls" his every move, citing only negative consequences for the American people. And did the media criticize Obama/Biden when he implemented 75 tariffs against China? Never once.

As one businessman explained it, in order to do business in China, the company has to turn over 51% of that business to the Chinese government. 51% gives the government, not the business, control over the firm in China. They then steal the technology, as with the company Apple, use it to start their own Chinese company, offering products (like the Chinese Opel phones) to their own people. Apple, in this example, does not benefit from the sales or trade, but was used and abused by the Chinese government. Because of this practice, many companies have left or are leaving China for other locations, such as Vietnam or Malaysia, where those governments offer more favorable practices. Leaving the deceptive Chinese government controls to other countries, then results in lower cost of goods for American consumers. The media does not report or explain this either.

The tariffs are a negotiating tool, with the end result in a better deal for the American consumers. The bias and false reporting by much of the media is why President Trump refers to them as "fake news".

Yes, free speech is not to be infringed upon, but when the rights of one are effected by the misleading or wrongful reporting of slanderous information, that is wrong.

Slavery in America

Throughout human societies, power and control over others is a dark side of our nature. Hence slavery, or the compulsion and control over other people have been a plague not easily cured. America started its young Statehood with slave ownership as a normal part of daily life. Through the struggles of history and blood, the ownership over people had been stopped by constitutional decree. But has it really?

According to studies and reports of world activities on the subject of slavery, there are about 40 nations that practice and allow the ownership of people. America is on that list. The idea of slavery is not just physical ownership, but also through control. Someone who is controlled by another, is that not also slavery, or a form thereof? Control is the drug of the powerful. Throughout history, it was those in power, the rich, the government, the military, and the politicians that made the rules and laws to control people. Some rules are for the benefit of society as a whole, other regulations are made to increase or hold the power of the elite class. As groups or leaders grow in power, the end result is control. Control leads to restriction, and restriction more often is of rights and liberties, leading to eventual slavery.

Which is which can be determined by the constitution, although the interpretation for modern application becomes debatable. If not stated or with precedence, then a law or ruling may be impeding on our rights. As that pertains to voting, for instance, does that restrict our freedom of speech? What about voter ID laws? The democrat party has been caught over and over manipulating election results by new ballots suddenly appearing after a close race, fake voter registrations, false mail-in ballots, and other deceptions. Perhaps voter laws are necessary in the dishonest world we live in, but one can argue that it is a way to restrict that right.

In America today, there are news stories where people are held against their will as slaves (often for personal pleasures), but for the most part, slavery as we define it, is very rare. Not absent in this country, news stories do arise about slavery. "Human Trafficking" across our southern border with Mexico is a grim reality that slavery in America is alive. Even in America, children are kidnapped and sold into slavery, but that also is never reported by the media.

In a sense, the major cities in America might be considered large slave plantations. The major cities, like San Francisco and New York, are now best known for "urination, defecation, needles and drugs", instead of the "the San Francisco Treat", or "the Big Apple". Look at the reports of rats and decay in Baltimore, the rampant gun violence in Chicago, and the crime and depravity in other cities. Why? Democrats have controlled the cities for decades, making promises every election cycle, doing nothing, and then asking to be reelected in the next election. This is true, look at any major city and who controls it, and check the status of poverty, crime, jobs, and any other metric, and how the people are doing. This is factual, look it up.

The inner cities especially, controlled by years and years of corrupt democrat leaders, have kept the poor (often African-Americans) in a state of slavery. Wasn't it the democrats who were the slave-holders of the south, during the American Civil War? Now, they have a stranglehold on the major cities, but the media never covers this. Instead, the media supports the democrat incumbents, without fair or honest reporting of the facts to the electorate. Where is the outcry of the "social warriors", the ACLU, and Black Lives Matter? They all profess the needs of the poor in the inner cities, yet do nothing to help them? It is because they support the system.

It is reasonable to argue that there are other forms of slavery being widely practiced in this country, such as by the banks. If you are in debt, you work as a slave to the bank to try and pay back what is owed. Financial slavery might be considered a type of control over people. It was of personal liberty to become indebted, but to some, it is involuntary servitude.

Those who struggle with addictions are slaves to that control source. There is a huge mess with control substances in our society, and a large volume of the filth comes across our southern border with Mexico. This has gone on for decades, where politicians make unfulfilled promises, and the media uses a "bait and switch" trick to turn our attentions elsewhere. There are huge profits made for the gangs and corrupt public servants, from the importing of illegal substances, which is clearly a form of slavery.

Governmental control by rules and regulations, may not quite be considered slavery, but as more of our rights get stripped away, then we can become slaves to the government, under legal means. In a society where the government controls the media and speech, the economy, and the conduct of virtually everything in life, personal choice does not exist, so isn't that slavery also? Yet, the democrats, various hate groups, and the younger generations are more vocal about wanting a socialistic society.

Look at the various debates and controversies mentioned today, and ponder whether our rights are being threatened, or society is positively fostered. Are the freedoms and liberties enhanced or preserved as guaranteed by our founding Fathers, or restricted by ever more restrictive laws crafted by leaders.

To be bold, look at many of the subjects people talk about. How about marriage and legal relationships? Do laws restrict or enhance "the pursuit of happiness"? If ones actions does not infringe upon another's' right, then constitutionally, maybe it's fine. Do voter laws suppress your right to vote? What would be reasonable in assuring "fair and free" elections? Are hate-speech laws lawful? What would constitute "hate", a differing opinion? Too much is being litigated these days because a group or persons finds "offense" or "bad feelings" because of the words of another person. Talk is talk, but when it comes to laws, that sounds more like the suppression of free speech, which is censorship.

How about gun laws and restricting the Right to bear arms? The intent of the Founders was to assure that the people would be able to defend themselves and their families from harm, and, to oppose a government that was unjust (tyrannical according to the document). Any infringement made by government is a violation of our rights. Don't accept the lies argued to the contrary. The Bill of Rights has this as the number two in importance for a reason, it's important.

The democrat party is more so strongly in favor of increasingly greater gun control than the republican or independent parties. As they lean more and more to a socialistic government controlled society, individuals with firearms are a threat. If the people are disarmed, then they are easily controlled. Again, look at history. What happened in Germany when the National Socialist party gained power? They seized the firearms of private citizens. The rest is history. Look at every nation that restricted or ended the private ownership of guns. The government had no opposition to impose its will on the people.

Remember the American Revolution? Way back in ancient American history, before Al Gore invented the internet, America was a group of independent colonies controlled by the English crown. Because the people had firearms, they were able to resist the control of the British government. If there were no weapons available, there would not have been any revolt, and no American nation today.

Important to note, there are great lengths happening right now in this country to control these rights, and that spells the end of American liberty, and ushers in the destruction of this nation. Watch and glean from every news story, every speech made, every law and action taken, to see if our freedoms are being upheld or restricted.

Political Parties - Flipping Red to Blue

The new democrat party aligns itself to bold speech with no substance. The party for the people is no more. The new party uses violent speech and divisive rhetoric to stir up the masses of brainwashed zombies to overthrow society, on every issue of tradition, law, and freedoms. The new party professes the goodness of socialistic ideals, no support for the rights of life, but whitewashes the realities of repeated historical failures. Condemnation without solution. The "Peoples Party" is no longer the party of the people, but by Elitists, pushing to overturn the rights of gun ownership, free speech, worship, the rule of law, and equality for all. They are indoctrinating of our school children with the ideas that "government provides", versus hard work, family tradition, and merit through achievement.

This radical departure of traditional norms relates exactly to every election, where more and more districts and States are turning blue. Turning blue, or democrat, was not a bad thing, but the Kennedy-era Democrat, the working man's party is long gone. The general populace is being brainwashed by empty promises that touts restriction and control, unsubstantiated opinion over logic and reason. Yet the vote turns blue, more and more often. It's like in the movies, when the people change from normal to zombies, and the power of the individual is given over to mass hysteria.

If this country is to be changed, let it be changed, through the process of law as it was founded. But what is changed, may not be what is good or right, or fair. And what changes, is not easily changed back. If traditions are deemed wrong, and what we have previously known as failed ideologies become entrenched, then individual liberties are restricted. The new rule of law becomes contrary to those established by our forefathers, and that seems to embrace evil over what we used to call good. And as power becomes concentrated in the hands of a few, there is no freedom of worship, freedom of speech, or anything else. Power is given over from the people (the individual), to the elites in government.

Who, or what groups adhere to what you hold as good and right? What you believe in, and the rights and privileges you enjoy, are just a few votes away from being changed. Think for yourself, and decide in the way that works best for you. Align yourself with those that hold those principles and ideals you want. And of course, pray. Pray for wisdom.

The Election of Californication

Just because what was, should never imply that something will remain. Pride or delusion can be a strong drink, but the truths and realities of this world have a sneaky way of catching even the best of people off guard. The results of the 2018 midterm elections was alarming from the perspective that democrat turnout was very high. The democrat Blue Wave, as it was called in the media, was successful in winning many more races than they should have. They won, or nearly won, as in many races, not because of the merits and experiences of the candidates, but rather from the marketing campaign that promoted them. They also won in a few races using dirty tricks. Documented cases where democrat election officials would stuff the ballot boxes with fake or duplicate votes, the mysterious mega-volume of "uncounted" ballots suddenly appearing after the election was decided, false voter registration, and other scams are used more often in recent elections.

Traditional influences on voters, like jobs, economy, family, or faith, are no longer the driving principles many voter segments care about. If so, with the great economic rebound, and the successes President Trump has had (despite the media lies), one would forecast that republicans should have won by vast margins. That was just not so, the wins were marginal at best. Depending on the voter groups or segments, they care about different optics. Whether it is of hyped rhetoric, or emotional dribble and fear, many groups vote based on superficial perceptions. Facts and realities don't assure votes any longer.

Now what is so wrong and bad about Democrat Blue? "That is a biased and 'racist' statement. "Only dumb religious fanatics, and red-neck Walmart shoppers would say such things, obviously they are degenerate deplorable Republicans." What difference does it make if a county or state is Blue or Red, democrat or republican, that's just politics. At the end of the day, people are just trying to get through the day, free to do their own thing. Who should care which political party is in office, it has nothing to do with daily life." What? Who should care? All of us. It comes down to personal choice versus government edict. Think about it.

That is the whole point, it makes all the difference! It makes a difference who leads us. The values and principles our leaders have, and how every aspect of our daily lives is influenced by governmental policy and laws. All of that matters to Christians and most Americans. To what point can or should government dictate what "we the people" should, do, think, or act? How is it, that a select group of leaders, rule over how we regulate our family values and beliefs? How can our elected leaders cower to the arm-twisting tactics of radical anti-life, anti-family groups like Planned Parenthood, that uses public taxpayer money to lobby and bribe politicians to enact abortion laws?

Because we are not standing up and getting our votes cast. We are not joining with other people and groups to support candidates and sound values. If we don't like the laws, we need to elect leaders that hold to more sound principles. I we don't stand for our values and the constitution, all of rights and freedoms will be gone.

A Blue America

The end game is this: a democrat controlled Washington, forever. The new democrat platform values government-sponsored, government-influenced, government control, of every aspect of American life, including reproduction and what a woman can or can not do with her body. In other words, a socialist or totalitarian America. No rights, no guns, limited speech, regulation and restriction, and individual liberty is dead. This is real and starting to happen, especially in the media and the public school system.

The current democrat party is wrought with socialistic ideals of government dependence and influence over the masses. The Kennedy-era Democrats are gone, or what is left in the party, are dead silent. There are moderate and conservative democrats. There are many good and decent Democrats who are pro-life. Does anyone ever hear a peep from them? Their party won't allow them to voice any dissenting opinion, and the fake news media never tells anything of them. Those good honorable people are puppets of the radical left wing of the party. Do we want them to regain power in Washington? "Kiss your guns goodbye."

Again, recall the Obama/Biden/Biden era. Eight years of governmental regulations, weak and decimated business and economic freefall, increasing taxes that drained your hard-earned resources, government failure to provide the promised health care, weak and disrespected influence worldwide, and division between the diverse peoples that make up America.

What did they do for illegal aliens and our gun laws? What was ever mentioned of the gun scandals, giving guns to the Mexican gangs, or the trade tariffs implemented with China. Remember how the democrat leadership was anti-Christian, anti-Israel? Look at the Johnson Law (if that's correct) where a pastor could not speak out about politics or politicians in the pulpit. Wasn't that a violation of our 1st Amendment rights? Exactly as mentioned earlier, but it was in fact happening. The Obama/Biden/Biden era, was a leftist, near socialistic government takeover that was moving to void every right and freedom we are suppose to have. This is just a foreshadow of the things to come, if we the people don't get active and elect good leaders. Compare then to now.

Rather than assess or describe a candidate, look at their records of how they have handled the affairs of the people. How do each of the democrats (and republicans); deal with the economy and taxes, national sovereignty, and protection of the citizens. How well did each handle health care, education, immigration and borders, protecting the rights and freedoms guaranteed under the Constitution? What was or is the stance in regards to guns, the constitution, church, life, and abortion? Of those principles that you value, how did each of these candidates fare? These are questions that should be asked at every election, for every candidate, regardless of party affiliation.

The Clinton era started this country on a downward spiral of the democrat party. With each successive candidate and leader, the party platform, their principles have moved further and further away from mainstream democrats, and most Americans. With every scandal, corruption, and dirty laundry exposed, it has turned away the masses of would-be democrat supporters; hence they supported Trump in 2016. Certainly, this may be greatly generalized, but to the average voter, Christian, republican, conservative, or other, the democrat party has greatly changed, and not for the better.

Voters can be swayed and convinced by the barrage of media and promises that candidates spew. The Kennedy-era generation is gone. Now the Millennials, the Generation-X, the younger voters, are easily bamboozled by social media hype and the fake biased news. The younger voter blocks are influenced by less than traditional values, and educational indoctrination by social activist teachers. Are they moved by candidate policies or promises? Perhaps they are more interested in the "feelings" and superficial things like the promises for free education, free health care, and free money, that gets their attention.

"Kudos" to the democrat party voter outreach programs, it has been very successful in mass marketing. They reach out and follow up on interested voter prospects far better than any republican machine.

And the republican base is getting old. The ol' reliable republican base is changing, getting beyond voting age or ability, with poor outreach to the younger generation or the new citizen bases. The republican public image is that of old tired white men, supported by big business, and the pursuit of wealth. Family values and tradition doesn't register with the younger voters, especially as the decline in marital commitments continues to plummet, leaving disenfranchised families. The younger generations are more tolerant of anything other than restrictive Christian churchy dogma. And a biased media deflates any positives that republican leaders make, and exonerates the new democrat values over truth and impartiality.

About Losing Our Liberties

Is it possible to lose our Constitutional rights and freedoms? These are guaranteed under the law, aren't they? This is America, the land of the free, isn't it? Yes, but no.

With each election, it results in more radical thinking politicians taking office, by which they get laws and regulations passed to silence free speech, for instance. Not so long ago, one could talk openly of another person or a group of people, have heated opposing debate, but that now is limited by "hate speech laws" and other controls. Yes, for sure it is not nice or kind to talk ill of another person or group, but can we not speak what's on our mind anymore? What if you spoke against a government agency or a governmental employee? Laws are being passed to limit what you can say against the government. What was accountability of government by the people, laws are starting to restrict that opposition, which can bring about serious consequences.

The silencing of open discussion, debate, or defiance, is control of our liberty. Some politicians seek control over us by enacting more laws and regulations in every area of our lives. Learn who the candidates are before you vote. Does the party platform, their set of ideals, align with your own, and how you want to live?

If democrat politicians (who have the mission to control the lives of the people) are elected, they will enact laws to reduce or eliminate the rights and privileges we hold, in particular our freedom to speak in opposition, our rights to bear arms, and the rule of law. As we lose our freedom of speech (again as an example), we become slaves to the government. If you are discontent with things now, wait until you have no choice at all!

Don't the republicans seek control also? Yes, sure they do, as all who are elected are subject to the lusts of power and control. It's just that in recent times, the democrat party has become so radical in their quest to control people by restrictive laws and regulations. Is that right or even fair? Some think it's fine, others are less happy, but the movement towards a socialist and totalitarian slavery will end the liberties and freedoms we still have. Some say, this country is just one election cycle away of this change.

This trend in our elections and the types of people elected to office is actually very scary. Too many are pushing for a government led, governmental controlled society. All countries that have embraced that style of slavery, are unproductive, with a people that are miserable, no incentive to do anything, just mindless robots. Those nations, historically, have not remained very long.

Other Freedoms to Lose

Freedom to speak out and speak freely, is not the only right and freedom we can lose, but all of the others as well. They are inter-related, one effects the others.

Gun rights are greatly threatened too. It is said the Second Amendment guarantees all of the others. Think about it, it is true. The Second Amendment protects the citizens' right to bear arms, for personal and family protection, but also to stand against tyrannical rulers. This fight has escalated in recent years, flamed by the biased media, and outspoken elitists. Here too, the critics claim that having guns is unsafe, yet those individuals have armed security and walled homes. Like every other argument the leftists scream about, they hold themselves above as being more knowledgeable or better than everyone else. These people use a double-standard, hypocrites, by example.

It was largely due to the influence of democrat leadership that established "gun free zones", places where the average law-abiding citizen can not carry a firearm Like schools or public buildings). In theory that sounds fine, but criminals don't obey laws, that's why they are criminals. Every mass shooting in recent history, has been in these "gun free zones". It is like telling a potential criminal, "come here, there will be no one to stop you." And this is true. In a gun free zone, only law enforcement, private sanctioned security, and criminals, have firearms. Whereas the regular citizen is trusting of the government to protect them, response time in a crisis incidence is slow, resulting in many deaths and injuries.

In a non-gun free zone, the potential for a trained citizen to protect themselves, or stand up in the defense of others, is much greater, making crime less likely. This is factual, shown by years of statistical information held by law enforcement and government sources like the FBI. When guns are present, in the hands of regular citizens, crime is less. That is true.

As you look at the history of every nation that has turned socialist, the first thing the government would do is to remove the guns. Remove the ability of the citizens to fight against injustice, and the people will be easily controlled. Remove the guns, and all other rights and freedoms can not be defended. Again, take Nazi Germany for example. There was strong active opposition to the rise of the socialists, but once the guns were seized, the Nazis eliminated all of the critics. And we are talking about the government killing its own citizens. It is that scary.

With every shooting, the democrats, in particular, scream for more controls, confiscation of weapons, and other limitations. Ammo taxes get added, taxes on firearm sales are increased, political arm-twisting gets certain models of firearms restricted or banned, and more rules and laws to limit our rights. But how does that reduce the crime level? It doesn't, it increases it likelihood.

Those people are calling for more registration, which becomes databases of gun owners. Then having lists of people, when gun confiscation does come about, they are easy to find. One trick to further restrict gun ownership is to increase taxes, then increase them again and again. Eventually, it becomes cost-prohibitive to own a gun. Or, if you don't pay the tax, the government can seize your firearms.

Another sneaky way the socialists are coming after gun owners is through the marijuana laws. Most states now make it legal to grow, own, or use marijuana, in varying degrees, as per state laws. The constitution reads that no one mentally incapable, or deemed medically incapable, can own or possess a firearm. That is basically what the founding fathers state. Well if most states now have laws allowing the long-time illegal drug use, then the government can then enact laws disallowing gun ownership if you are a marijuana smoker, or even for medical purposes. Then, the government can legally seize your firearms.

Instead of trying to remove the Second Amendment, which is all but impossible to do right now, all the anti-gun folks need to do is get more restrictive laws enacted. Many states now have "Red Hat" or "Red Flag" laws. That is, a state or local law whereby the local lawman can seize your guns without "due process". They are based on the idea, that verbal hearsay, not factual evidence, can trigger a seizure. If you don't like your neighbor, or have a political rival, then call the sheriff and claim that person is a threat.

Think about it. The more these groups seek ways to restrict gun ownership, and mass registration, the eventual outcome will be confiscation. Take away the guns, and the people will be under the control of the government.

More about the First Amendment

The First amendment to the US Constitution was basically two issues, the rights of free speech, and the rights to freely worship. The free speech side has been extensively looked at, but what about the freedom of religious worship?

Here also, religious teachings are also in the center of controversy these days. Speech and religion are the first and most important rights the founders declared. Why, that was what the English rulers suppressed most. You must not restrict free thought or personal preference of spiritual worship. That also includes the fight over abortion. What is life, the handling of "the pursuit of happiness" in conflict with religious belief, speech, and law? Laws are words spoken by men. Some are for the good of the nation and its citizens, others are for the power and gain of some leaders. When government enacts laws to restrict either speech or religion, that is wrong.

America was borne on the rock of Our Judeo-Christian heritage. Examine every writing of most of the founding fathers, and it is clear that most were men of stout Christian faith. From our Christian roots, every freedom and right we hold are Biblical ideals. Our Constitution and our entire legal system, are based on our religious beliefs. And these days, the Christian faith, in particular, has been greatly under attack as well.

We are free to worship whom and what we like, or nothing at all, without the interference of government mandating what we can do. The idea of "separation of Church and State", has been grossly portrayed by those seeking to abolish Christianity. Thomas Jefferson and Hamilton had written about this matter from the beginning, citing that "not separation, but rather that "government shall not impose a religion". In other words, government would not declare a "State religion". Being a person of faith, whatever you believe, and part of the government structure, should not be an issue. It is, and watching every Supreme Court nomination hearing, and even most Cabinet level screenings, there are those people, mostly the democrats, that scream about the separation of Church and State. Having a person that holds a belief and moral compass in public office is a good thing. Look at the corrupt lying filth currently serving in office, and then decide which is better.

Through many great struggles, those that claimed the "separation of church and State" pertained to our public school system, prayer, and the teachings of faith had been stripped in the 1960s. Many of the early schools and universities had Christian roots, and the Bible was often the sole book available to teach children. As the support of faith is pushed out from public arenas, the quality of education, has turned increasingly poor, with our children having no sense of a moral compass. In our school system today, the mention of Christian faith is highly condemned, often with disciplinary action. But the mention of non-Christian thinking is praised. Is that not a restriction of our rights to worship? If ones actions do not interfere with the rights of another, then it is legal.

And what about "the right to life"? The abortion question, is not just a freedom of religious worship, but it is also a freedom of speech. It may be that quasi notion, the "Pursuit of Happiness". Perhaps the greater overall question is whether it is right and lawful for the government to kill, or sanction the killing, of its own citizens. Although the Supreme Court allowed the ability to kill unborn babies as a rule of law in Roe vs. Wade, is it right? No, it is a disgusting and abhorrence to everything good and honorable that this country touts to be. Murder is murder. An unborn child is still a human being, up until now.

The State of New York, Virginia, and Vermont have passed new laws allowing the death of babies right up until the child takes its first breath. And, the voting members applauded the new law with resounding glee! It is said that liberty will die with resounding applause. Are we there? Whether life begins at conception or when a baby draws its first breath, is irrelevant. The question is, how can we as a nation allow the murder of our own innocent and defenseless citizens? We are suppose to be a nation ruled by law, but not all laws are good or just. Where is the sanity of our lawmakers? This is murder, plain and simple.

Now if this hennas debauchery of injustice is not overruled, then the rights of free speech, religious worship, and "the pursuit of happiness", are made mute. Our freedoms, as guaranteed under the US Constitution, are destroyed. Those lawmakers, supporters of such legislation, and any group or organizations that adheres with such, are murders plain and simple. Is this country really going down this path? Then truth and justice in America is a lie!

What follows next? Well, because the murder of babies is made legal, the next step is to broaden that "definition" of whom can be (legally) murdered. Next will be young children no longer wanted by their parents, perhaps the elderly will be killed because they area burden to society. Then from there, any opposition group or segment of citizens might be legally murdered, like white males, Christians, deplorable republicans, and so on. "When the sword is unsheathed, it is difficult to put it back without first spilling blood." When a nation slinks into the depravity of celebrating and condoning death, then its end is near.

If speech is restricted, by laws or groups, and gun are taken away (or further restricted), and the rights to assemble in our churches is then limited, then we have no freedoms left. And when the government is allowed to restrict your rights to own a firearm, or takes them away completely, then there will be no more questions about religion, free speech, abortion, rights to assemble, protests against the government, and so on. "Those who gain power will abuse it, then they will oppress the people, which then they will start murdering the citizenry (by law)." Strongly ponder these thoughts.

Make a Difference

Your vote does count. Your vote is your voice. It's a liberty and a right that must not be silenced or impeded by opposition, or by the government. To allow your voice to be shut down, you lose the one easy, and best, freedom a citizen can hold. "Use it or lose it", is a cliche sometimes used, and it is applicable now. Voting is your decision, takes a stand, either "for" or "against", but voice your opinion, it does matter.

Our government was founded on the principle that if people are left to live their lives freely, society grows and prospers, supported by happy citizens. Creativity and invention, improvements of life, make for a better world. As simplistic as that sounds, basically it's true.

Our system of government was designed and set up to assure the people would have the liberty to become all they can aspire to do. The freedom of free and open speech has been the cornerstone of the greatness this country has shared, rooted in the process of free and open elections. Every vote counts, and every citizen has a duty to make this country better, according to their own conscience.

The importance of your vote, which is your voice, should be expressed, even now, and especially for this upcoming election. If you can physically do so, do vote. As mentioned previously, whether you like a particular party or candidate, or a person seeking reelection, let your voice be heard. You right is also not to vote, which is your free decision. But , is surrendering your voice by not voting, is to submit to the will of someone else.

As our society writhes with turmoil and unrest, forces of change come about, heading towards a revolution or major upheaval of our liberties. And in this country, at this moment in time, many people and groups, seek to undermine our rights to vote, our power of speech, all of our other freedoms and liberties we still have. That would sound the death-blow to America.

About the Author

I grew up in a middle class family, had a father that worked, a mother that stayed home and raised children, the typical traditional American home. We had a small house, one car, (no) white picket fence, we had pets, regular schooling, church-goers, watched news and various TV shows, and had all of the cliche normal things in life typified during the 1950s and 60s. Life was normal and decent, reasonably peaceful, and safe.

My father was a veteran, worked a blue collar job, and was a straight-line democrat, just like his father before him. The Kennedy era thinking of party politics was pretty much his thinking as well. And for many decades, that seemed to work well in America. I too learned and adopted similar ideas of how life and government should work and coexist.

But that has changed radically over the past couple decades as the democrat party is no longer the party of the average working man. One would best describe the party as what we used to call the Communist-Socialist party during that earlier era. Now the party is all about hate speech, bigotry, division, dirty-politics, rampant dishonesty and deception by party leaders and candidates, and everything revolving around government control. This is no longer the democrat party America once loved.

The candidates and false narratives they promoted were enough to make me switch parties. Over the last many election cycles while the democrats drove further left, I pushed my family and friends to switch parties and vote further right. Not that the republicans are perfect by any means, but they do hold to more of the values and principles I do. The biggest area where they align with my own thinking are the ideas of limited government, a government hands-off ideology, and support of the Constitution and the foundations of this country. Upholding our rights and freedoms are more their forte, so this is where we will stay.

My hope is to share these thoughts with you, so that you can glean some insight of the struggle we face over our dying liberties. Thank you reading this.

Also consider these other books written about our Rights and Freedoms. These also are found on Amazon Kindle under the Politics section. Look for:

"The Democrat Blue Wave is the Zombie Apocalypse"
by T. H. Logwood
ASIN: B07MYBFKT1

* * * * *

The American Civil War II
By T. H. Logwood
ASIN: B08CQ4PDMQ.

* * * * *

Don't Tread on Me
By T. H. Logwood
ASIN: B07X5DRRYB

* * * * *

I Met a Man Named Donald
By T. H. Logwood
ASIN: B0842YF1HH.

* * * * *

"The End of American Liberty"
by T. H. Logwood
ASIN: B07HPYZWTF

* * * * *

Repent America, In the Name of Jesus!
By T. H. Logwood
ASIN: B07NBXYLLB

* * * * *

The Democrat Blue Wave is the Texas 2nd Alamo
By T. H. Logwood
ASIN: B07N7N2WG6

* * * * *

"The End of American Freedom"
by T. H. Logwood

ASIN: B07MSJ4QD7

* * * * *

"The U.S.S. La Porte (APA 151), The Pearl of the Pacific"
by T. H. Logwood
ASIN: B07L6JXRB9